ANARCHIST
LOVE
POEMS

BY
SPERO THEMISTOCLES GARDIAKOS

ANARCHIST LOVE POEMS

2nd Printing.
Copyright 1999, 2021 Spero Themistocles Gardiakos

Original printing:
Aurora 1999
OBOL INTERNATIONAL
Div. UNIGRAPHICS INC.
63 S. Broadway
Aurora IL 60544

ISBN: 0-86723-013-4

SPERO THEMISTOCLES GARDIAKOS

A Brief Introduction

Hesperus is Phosphorus.

The slim volume of poetry before you was originally published in 1999, with poems written throughout the end of the teens years of the author. What contextually moves the sense and reference of these poems between the morning star and evening? What makes these poems at once a time capsule of being young in 1999 and also works meaningful enough to have them return to print after twenty two years out of print?

The author, Quechua Runa and Ἕλληνες, Hellenes, from Kalamáta, facing compulsory military service, raised between continents, dishoused by environmental and political disasters, quite naturally fronting a Punk band, Erebus, took time of quiet in noises places to write love poems to a sad world.

Think on a nineteen year old whose peers in the United States worried about getting a new car and this one's mind was full of Kurds, Cyprus, Palestine, Armenian Genocide, Indigenous Genocide, Indian Wars, Túpac Amaru, language preservation, and the seeming endless parade of brutality against the human experience.

And just so, he wrote love poems.

Enjoy these words in context. Find sense and reference in them. Be as aspirational as this young person tried so hard to put into words.

Micah Chaim Thomas

THERE'S NO FUTURE WITH THE FASCIST POWERS
THE KIDS ARE THE FUTURE
NEW SEEDS IN AN OLD FOREST…
BECOMING A JUNGLE
WE'RE THE FUTURE
YOUR FUTURE

Author's Foreword

First of all I want to thank my friend Micah, for pushing me to print my old poetry. I was very reluctant at first. Flattered yet mostly mortified that I have to share my feelings as a teen, with others. Having to look back and revisit myself at a young age, is always a shock. I hadn't read or even thought of any of these poems for over 20 years. For me the poems where my past, but to hear someone wanting to bring them back, I had to push my hesitation aside and say "fuck it".

I started writing at the age of 14 or 15, trying, like most teens, to find a way to express feelings we were never taught to deal with. Feelings of anger towards imperialist countries waging war on small and undeserving populations. The Balkans, Chechnya, Kurdistan to name a few. Feelings of anger towards injustice. Watching people starve, while people owned million dollar cars and yachts. Refugees pouring into Greece because of wars they never wanted, to make people they will never meet, richer. Like most teens, I just wanted to make sense of war, capitalism, imperialism and suffering a.k.a. the world we live in.

I was raised to believe I should be proud to be Greek; that I am superior because I am Greek, because of what people who died millennia before me had done, only to find xenophobia and hatred in my "superior" brethren, and to be constantly reminded that I am not, and never will be, a true Greek.

When I moved to Chicago I though my South American brethren would finally accept me as one of their own. And I would fit in. Sadly, I was never taught my mama's mother tongue, Spanish. This deprivation has cost me immensely for, what greater gift can be endowed on a child than having the linguistic tools to express oneself transculturally? This lack has also been weaponized against me by Latinos/Mestizos who rejected the notion that i was one of them. Once more I was acutely aware that I would not be accepted with arms open, by who I identified as my brethren.

After being harassed, assaulted, and abused by fascists, townies, racists and police in Greece, and police in the US, I found acceptance in the Chicago anarcho-punk movement; finding inspiration from the songs and lyrics of "Crass", a punk band from the UK.

Through them I found the courage to start a band and continue writing and fighting for a better world, and a better future. In their words: "The nature of your oppression is the aesthetic of our anger." That became my war cry.

Anger and screams being my only weapon as a young, angry teen, I was tired of being abused by the world, I fought back as a lead singer in a punk band.

Verses carry with them whole cultures, mindsets, zeitgeists! These little grenades were written by an outsider, trying to navigate this pulsating, bleeding world. So i present to you these poems of youth and eternal anarchy.

Many things have changed from 15 year old me to 42 year old me. This can be seen in the immaturity and naivety of my writing as a confused teen. Not that my writing style has changed much. I still write like an angry 15 year old. Yet my core beliefs have remained the same.

No love for any nation.

All government is force.

There is no authority but yourself.

Peace.
Love.
Anarchy.

Always,

Spero

ANARCHIST LOVE POEMS

<u>The Age of Cries</u>

In the age of the mighty dollar
In the age mankind has sought for

Two thousand years of culture
Two thousand years of sculpture

The time where man is free
The time where man can dream

We hope this is all true
We hope tyranny is through

Our eyes closed 'till we die
Our eyes torn out with a cry

Cries of freedom silenced
Cries dealt with violence

Freedom stolen from the womb
Freedom is said to be our doom

Can't control our human right
Can't give up without a fight

In the age of the might dollar
In the age I thought I sought for

SPERO THEMISTOCLES GARDIAKOS

<u>Death of the Sun</u>

The sun has died for good
The moon might not come out

The stars my only hope
The clouds cover them up

I ask the sun to stay
He tells me they won't let him

I ask the moon to stay
She says what they want her to

I ask the clouds to go
They say they must stay

I cannot see the stars
I cannot see my hope

The sun has died for good
The moon is dead now too

ANARCHIST LOVE POEMS

Government Suppression

If you are denied your freedom to protest
If you are denied your freedom to be alive
If you are forced to do things you don't like
If you are forced to fight for someone else

If you must wear chains so you can be free
If you are denied your given right of freedom
If you must conform so you may be different
If you cannot lead a normal free life

If your leaders don't want you to be free
If your soul is in jail for life
If they just don't let you be
If you feel like a gun's against your head

Then you should just fight the system
Then you should just change the system
Then you should just fight the system
Then you should just open your eyes

Break Through

Freedom does not mean terror
What you learned is just an error
Chaos doesn't join along
I'll try to tell you in this ode

Freedom is not at all destruction
Governments just bring corruption
They have just destroyed us all
Brought our souls and spirits down

Freedom is our given right
It is only within our sight
Cant be scared to live like men
Live like men or just be dead

Open your mind don't be scared
Queens and kings never cared
For you and me or anyone
Help fight back you're not alone

Destruction of our government
The people are in puzzlement
What to do in this world
The President is not our lord

Break right through your stone walls
Free yourself hear your spirit call
Tear your chains right off your arms
Try and reach one of the stars

Don't let them put you down no more
Don't let them make your life a chore
Standing there won't change a thing
Try and be a human being

ANARCHIST LOVE POEMS

USSA

I am the president of the USA
A fascist leader gonna blow you away
If you mess with us I'll press the button
Nuclear explosions will be very sudden

You country's not Christian enough
I can't protect nor have peace with your country
Anything you do offends my country
Can't let you harm my American foundry

I'll you away you communist scum
What you believe is really dumb
I'll you believe you have freedom of speech
Say the wrong words you'll be found in a ditch

I'll give you hopes for a better tomorrow
Of course, they're all lies pleases don't be sorry
The schools you go to are a little biased
Now one will know you're taught to be robots

I am a dictator controlling all
I rule a country that will never fall
Whoever denied me I'll put him in the chair
For what he did it's only fair

War and Hatred

Look into my eyes and see the sorrow
Since we all know there will be no tomorrow
Atomic power chemical power
That's why you won't see a flower

Kill your brother and your sister
Got a gun I'll see you later mister
Our graveyard is big enough
For all the suckers that die for us

Communism socialism monarchy too
They're the enemy shoot to kill
I've got to go fight for the sake of my country
Don't know why that's just what they told me

You've become a robot programmed to kill
Not to care or even feel
Your head is pumped full of shit
You hear something different and you get a fit

Genocide homicide infanticide too
Kill kill kill is all you do
Fight for this and fight for that
War has always been full of crap

ANARCHIST LOVE POEMS

<u>Ode to the Kurds</u>

Standing strong and powerful
Standing always true

Never ever falling back
Never giving in

Warriors always fighting back
Warriors with no chance

Honor is on their side
Honor is all theirs

The path of freedom's what they chose
The path of a great life

Back to Light

Darkness covers all the light
Darkness stays through the night

Enemies once were my friends
Four hundred times to defend

Powers beyond my comprehension
Lead them towards their defection

Bitter tears, the loss of friendship
Bitter taste on both of my lips

No more sorrow, no more hatred
No more fighting ,friendship's sacred

Thought that friendship was forever
Thought that hatred would be never

All I asked for is respect
What I asked for, didn't get

No more sorrow, no more mourning
No more fighting no more tearing

Time to get up face the facts
Time to take the knife out my back

Darkness stays through the night
Mornings coming, Finally there's light

ANARCHIST LOVE POEMS

Death

Don't be afraid to die
But don't be afraid to live
For life is short to be wasted
Life is not too far from death

Waking up no one knows why
Death just creeps from beyond
All the people that have gone
All the friends I have lost

The knife of pain won't come off
The blackened tears don't dry off
The sorrow like a tumor
The solitude won't surrender

Alone in a cell
Alone like an orphan
Alone like your friends
That won't enjoy any more

I realized that it's too short
I realized I will live now
Don't be afraid to die
Be afraid you won't really live

SPERO THEMISTOCLES GARDIAKOS

<u>Cut My Wings</u>

Since my eyes are glued down shut
And my wings have been cut off
You bastards come and fill me with
All these different lies

Take your knife from my back
Take those corks from my ears
Take your knife please from my heart
Take your nails from my hands

Will you stop screwing me over
Will you stop killing my freedom
Take your gun from my head
Take your arrow from my back

Take your chains from my feet
Take your sword from my lungs
Give me back my heart
Give me back my brain

Please don't take my soul away
Please don't take my beliefs
Please will you unglue my eyes
Please will you not cut my wings

ANARCHIST LOVE POEMS

Armageddon

It's time for you to die
To die because of God
It's time for the final battle
It's time for Armageddon

It's all the fuckin' same
We're all just human beings
What does religion matter
When blood spills on your hands

Holy wars and holy crap
Holy this and holy that
Don't believe in fake idols
Don't believe in myths

I believe in liberty
I believe in anarchy

Time for War

Death and destruction coming to your door
Death and destruction flying over your head
Dropping A-bombs on your head
Shooting pistols in head

War, war, and more war
Dead, death, and more death
Blood for them to drink
On the forgotten graves

Dying for your country and your morals
Dying for someone's big fat wallet
Dying to be a real big man
Forgotten tomorrow

ANARCHIST LOVE POEMS

Time to Go

You think you're brave
I think you're desperate
Are you ready then
To condemn
So many innocent lives
You'll get some money
If you ever come bac
But will you ever be able
To forgive yourself
For what you did
You have to fight they say
There is no other way
But do you really know
Why you must really go
To fight for freedom
That's not the reason
They just want money
And smaller countries
To bow before them
So then why ask when
You will go home at last
You think it'll be real fast
But no one remembers you
You think, was it worth it too?

The Struggle

My head up high
My spirit strong
I'll always try
The fight's real long

My soul is weakened
My heart is tired
But that's no reason
To kill the fire

My head is spinning
Am I winning
Or am I just losing

I'll keep on fighting 'till I die
I'll always fight against what's wrong
I'll always keep my spirit strong

ANARCHIST LOVE POEMS

<u>Stopped by the System</u>

Held back by the system
Not any more
Held back by the power
Of money and its whores
Shut off by religion
And their vengeful god
Outcast of society
With their fascists wars
They are the violence that parade down our street
They are the predators that prey on the weak
They are the rich ones that steal from the poor
They are the fascists that send us to war
We must stand together
Bring the system down
Stop brainwashing us
Lies in school must stop
We will wake you up
Make your dreams come true

SPERO THEMISTOCLES GARDIAKOS

No More Dependence

All they do is take and take
But they don't like to give
They say they give us freedom
But freedom they can't give
They say they give us liberty
But they don't know that liberty
Is not theirs to give

They want us to obey
But they never will repay
They like to give us crap
Throw us in the trash
Don't want us to get out
Don't want us to move free
So we will need them
They cut our feet and make us think
That we need them to move around
We can walk without them
We can fly without them

ANARCHIST LOVE POEMS

Betrayal

Tear my trustful heart out
Turn me inside out
Rip my destroyed head off
Cut my arms and legs
An orphan with no orphanage
A kid without a home
Treason of the highest sin
Back stab from your closest friend
Death sent from a god himself
Murder from a pacifist
Wake up call from Morpheus
Tyrant from an anarchist
Freedom stopped by the free
Unexpected circumstance
From People that I loved
The knife hurts even more
When you thought they cared
Hanging from the tallest tree
Pushed off by your own
Bullet in your own head
Shot by one of them
Betrayal of the highest form
Brought from ones you loved
The pain can only stop
When one of us has ceased
Living or deceased
The pain you gave to me
Is buried deep inside
My face is turned to shambles
My self-respect feels dead
My dignity is smeared all over
My soul is on the floor

SPERO THEMISTOCLES GARDIAKOS

<u>No More Regrets</u>

The shadows of the past
Keep the light from shinning through

The storms of history
Won't let the earth dry up

The skies of darkness
Like a blanket of regret

The roots are deep
Won't let the new trees grow

The light can shine when we help the sun
The earth can't live without the rain
The dark sky still has a moon and stars
New seed won't grow 'till the old one's killed

ANARCHIST LOVE POEMS

Listen to Your Soul

Hear the drumbeat of your heart
Hear it calling out for you
Hear it wanting you to fly
Hear it flying with your soul

Why are you not going with
Why are you still staying with
Why will you not help them fly
Why won't you let them soar free

If you don't you will be stuck
If you won't you cannot fly
If you stop them they won't soar
If you will not they will cry

Your heart was made for freedom
Your spirit's meant to soar
Your mind must do some thinking
Your soul was meant to fly

Last Chance

Life is only once
There's no second chance
Cannot turn time back
Life goes by too fast

Enjoy it while it's here
Enjoy it while you can
Try to do your best
Try to let it last

Realize what it's worth
Realize while you can
Don't let it slip right through
Don't let it fly away

This is all we get
It's our only shot
But once that it's all over
All is lost forever

ANARCHIST LOVE POEMS

Laughter of the Children

The wind blows through the blood red leaves
A whistling sound so calm and soothing
The birds that soar the birds that sing
A gorgeous song so perfect clean
The children play they run they laugh
Their voices make your heart feel light
The sun is warming full of power
Like a beautiful bright spring flower
My love is gorgeous like a princess
Such a perfect beauty, she's all I live for
But then they choose to kill it all
With their wars, their holy cause
To prove that they will rule it all
Just so all others will fall
The children silent laugh no more
Millions dead with all these wars
The birds might sing, the wind will whistle
Doesn't matter if there's no children to listen

Who Will Cry

Do angels cry with what they see
Do angels cry with the world we weave
Do angels cry when we kill
Do angels cry with what they see

The death the anger the hate that breeds
Like a sickness spreads through you and me
The vaccine is something called love
The cure is simple it just needs faith

Do people cry with what they see
Do people cry with the world we weave
Do people cry when we kill
Do angels care about you or me

ANARCHIST LOVE POEMS

Revenge Always Comes

All is paid back in this life
Nothing goes without revenge
No one gets away from life
All will pay for what they've done

You can't run from yourself
You can't run away from life
You can't run from what you've done
It'll catch up before you know

Twice the pain that you have caused
Twice the worries that I felt
Twice the anger of defeat
I will have my sweet revenge

Paths of Four Horizons

The four horizons bring many things
The different paths can confuse us
The many side streets no one knows
The true path may not be that easy

The path for freedom is not the first
The path for peace can be real tough
The path you choose, not always right
The path you choose can be deceiving

We've all chose wrong ones once
We've all made a wrongful turn
We've all been pointed the wrong way
We've all been misguided from our truths

What you choose is sometimes wrong
What you choose is sometimes right
What you choose is all that matters
What you fix will matter too

The four horizons bring up many things
The different paths confuse us all
The wrong path you chose can be corrected
The right path will again appear before you

ANARCHIST LOVE POEMS

<u>My Reason of Existence</u>

Our souls attached before time
Have been together always twined
Through the ages none will exist
Undying love that will not shift

Your eyes like magic to my heart
Your beauty with no end or start
Life was nothing before you
You showed me how to be true

My life fulfilled with you around
I love you so I scream out loud
Our lives together I hope will be
I want you forever, be with me

I'll give you anything you want
Cause you know you have my heart
The stars are yours if you wish
All I ask if for one sweet kiss

And if the day comes where I must die
Your face is all I need to smile
To hear you tell me, I love you
Then rest in peace and wait for you

SPERO THEMISTOCLES GARDIAKOS

<u>United We Win</u>

The sun that shines
The moon that glows
The stars are mine
And yours to hold

Together we will make a change
Together we will break the cage
Our strengths united we can't fail
Our strengths united can't be impaled

Learn from all our mistakes
Learn from all the risks we take
We will fight and shout out loud
We will change the world around

ANARCHIST LOVE POEMS

What Silence Tells Us

The dead don't speak of worldly horrors
They can't tell us of old mistakes
We can't imagine what they've lived
We only hope we're better off

We do not hear of all the wars
They don't tell us of all the hate
They don't tell us of the backstabbing
They don't tell us of the betrayals

We don't need to know their errors
We don't need to hear them talk
Their silence tells us what we need
Their future is our present now

IF YOU WANT A GOOD STRONG FLOWER
YOU MUST HAVE GOOD ROOTS
AND WATER THEM WELL
IF YOU WANT A GOOD STRONG FUTURE
YOU MUST TEACH THE CHILDREN THE TRUTH
AND NOT FILL THEM WITH HATE